Clear My Mind
Piano Book

The full piano score for all
twelve songs from Clear My Mind

Eric Elder

Cover image by Michael Swanson.
Used with permission.

Clear My Mind: Piano Book is one of
several inspirational resources produced by
Eric Elder Ministries, including a two-week
devotional book based on these songs called
Two Weeks With God. For more inspiring
books and music, please visit:

www.InspiringBooks.com

ISBN 978-1-931760-39-3

Table of Contents

Moment By Moment

Eric Elder

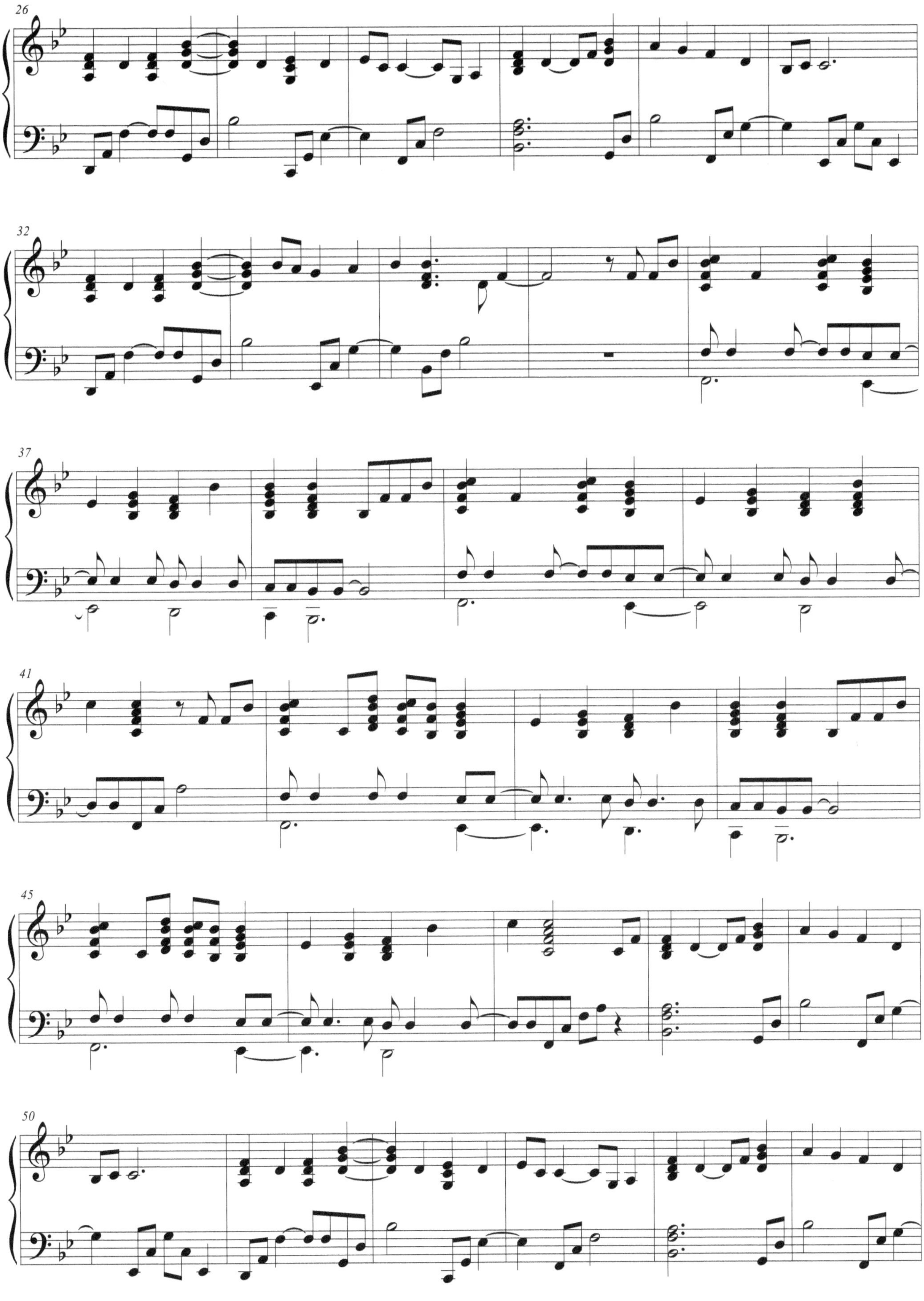
26
32
37
41
45
50

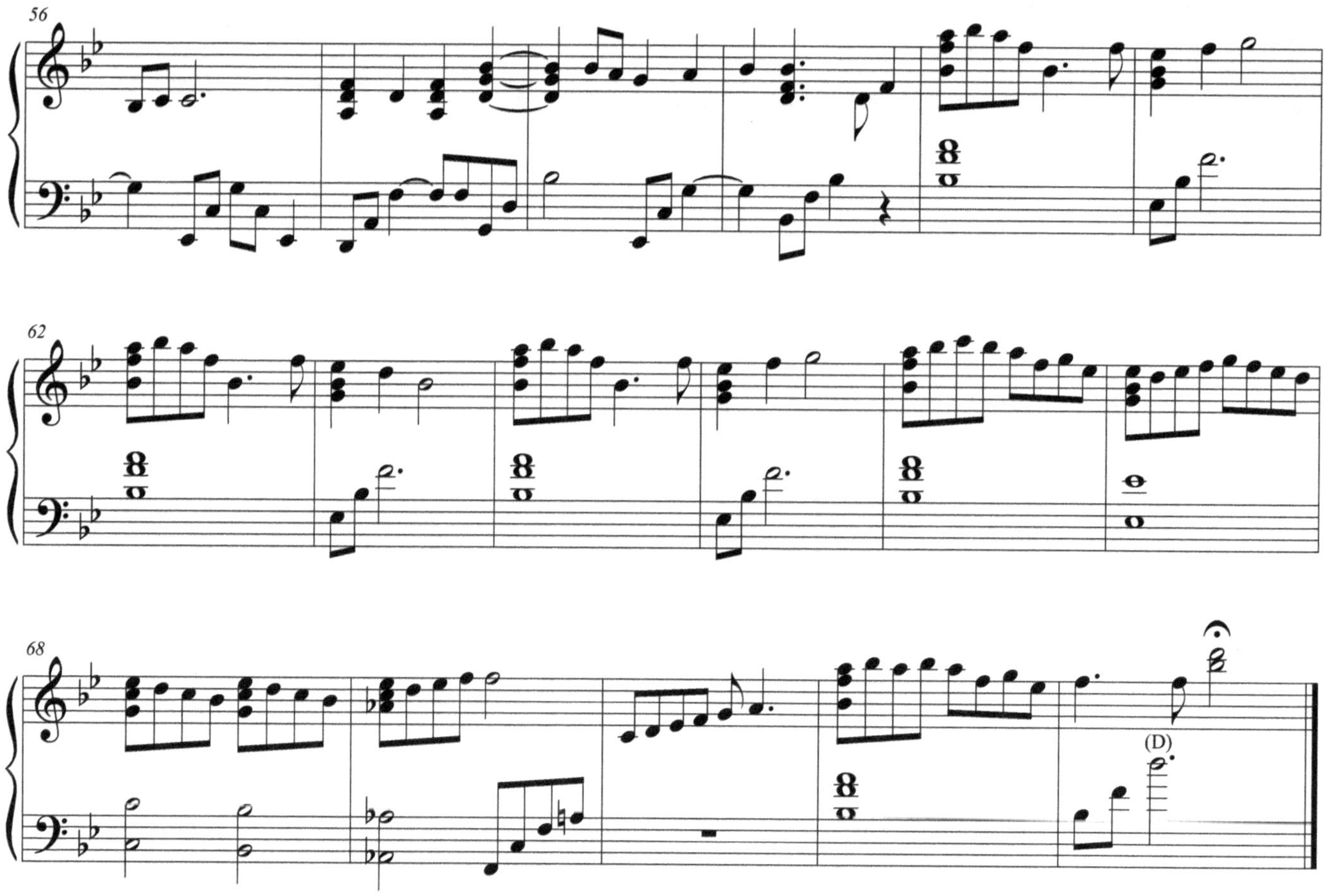
56
62
68
(D)

You Are The Way

Eric Elder

7

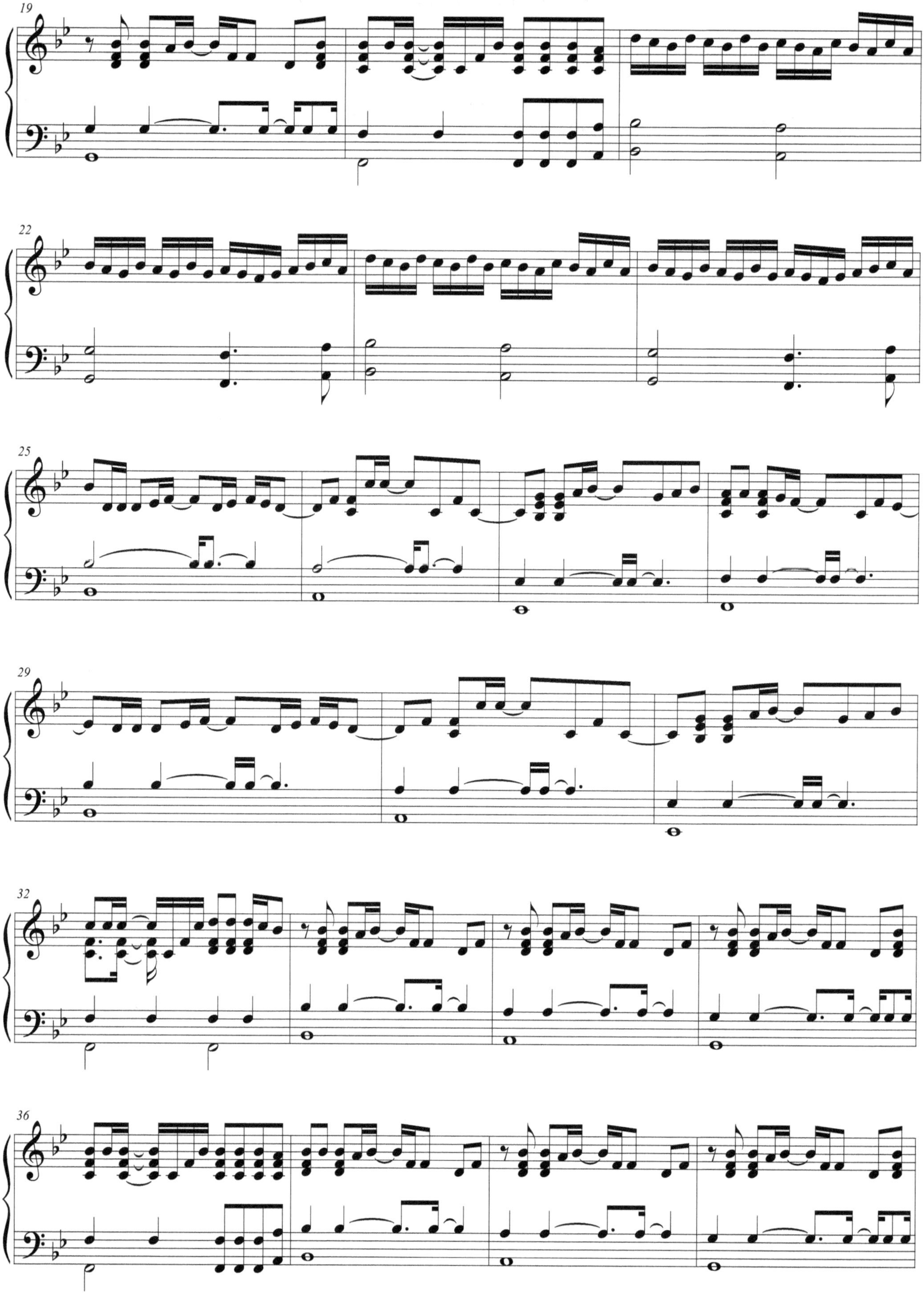
19
22
25
29
32
36

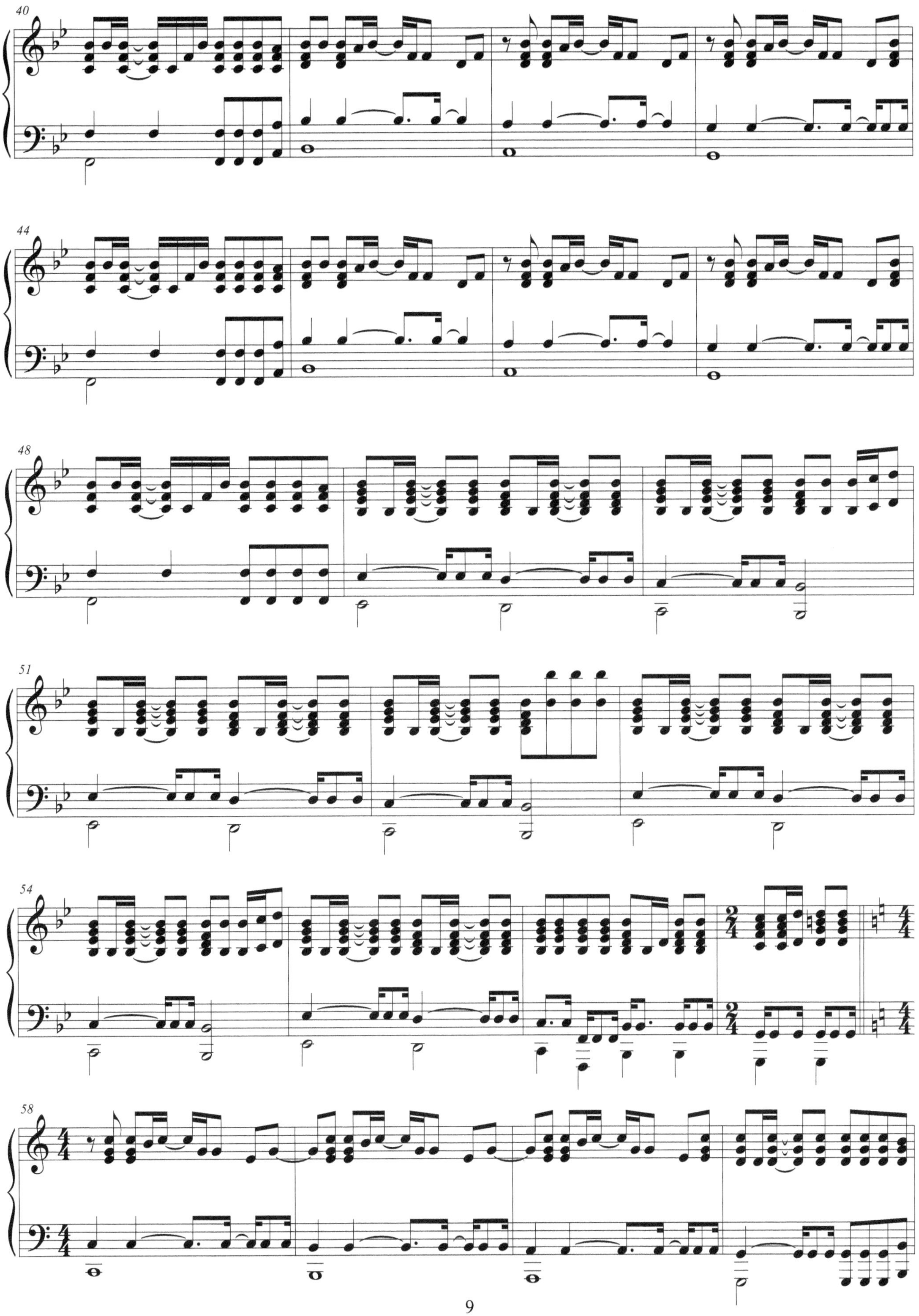
40
44
48
51
54
58

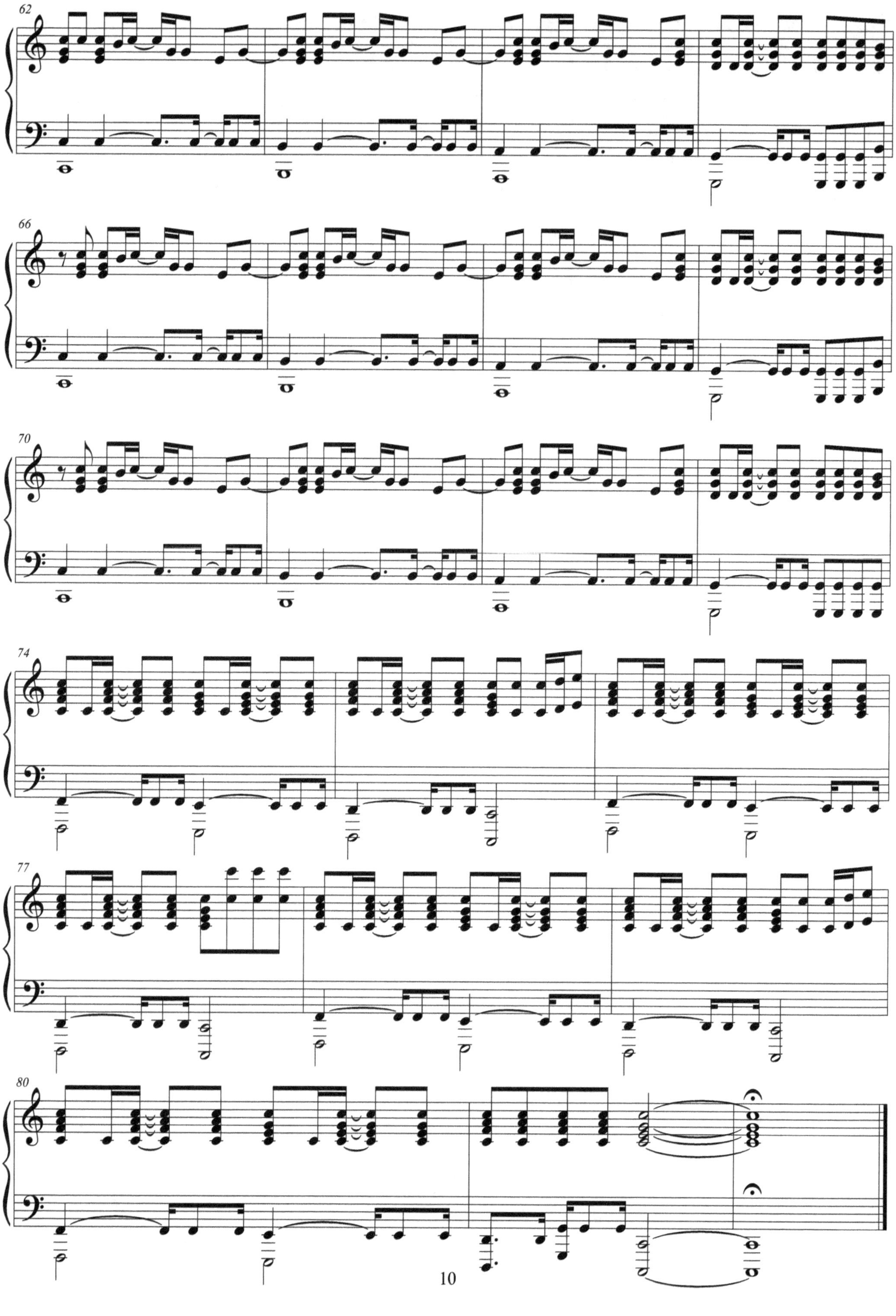
62
66
70
74
77
80

Go Into All The World

Eric Elder

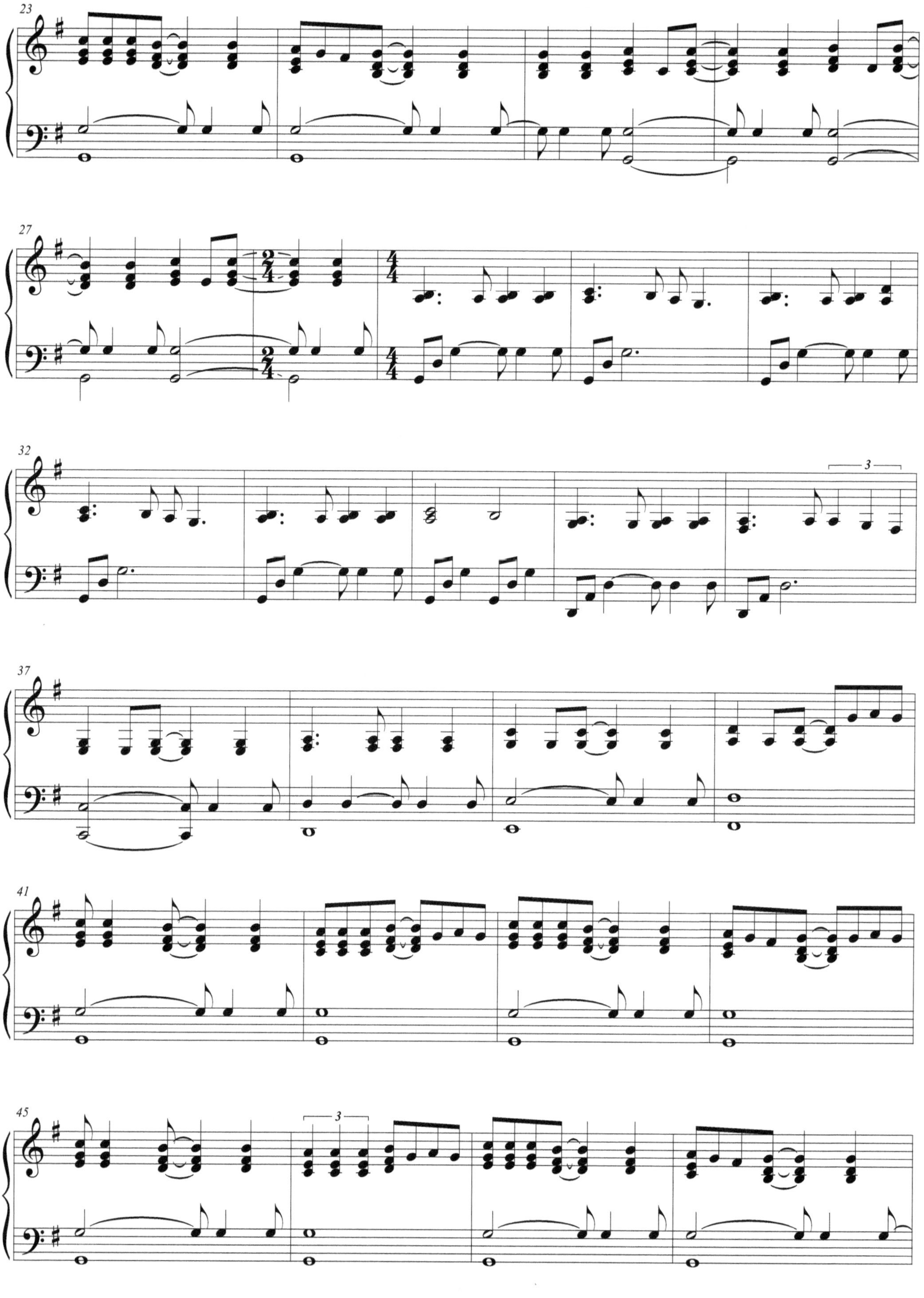
23
27
32
37
41
45
3

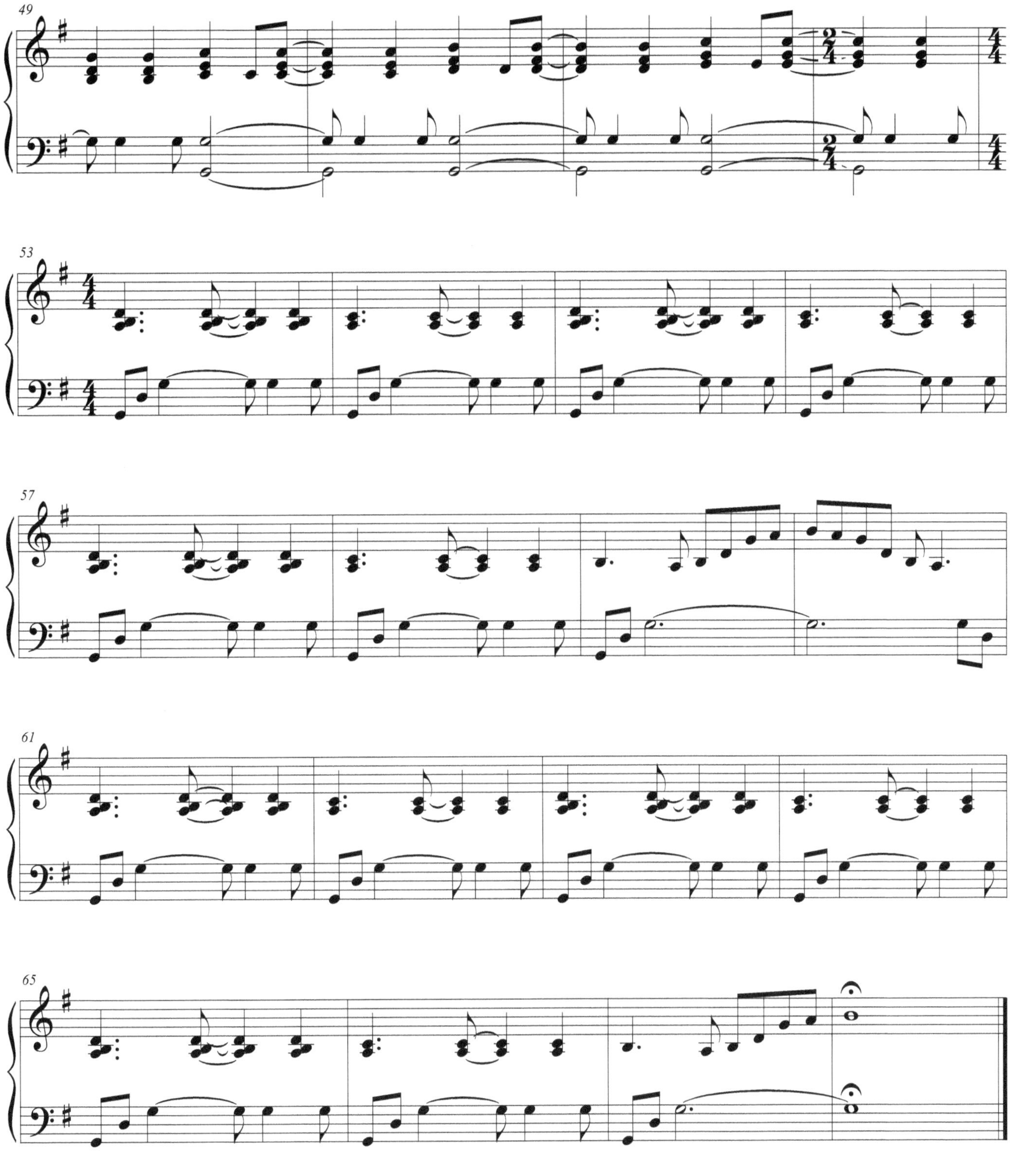
49
53
57
61
65

Stand On Me

Eric Elder

Stand On Me

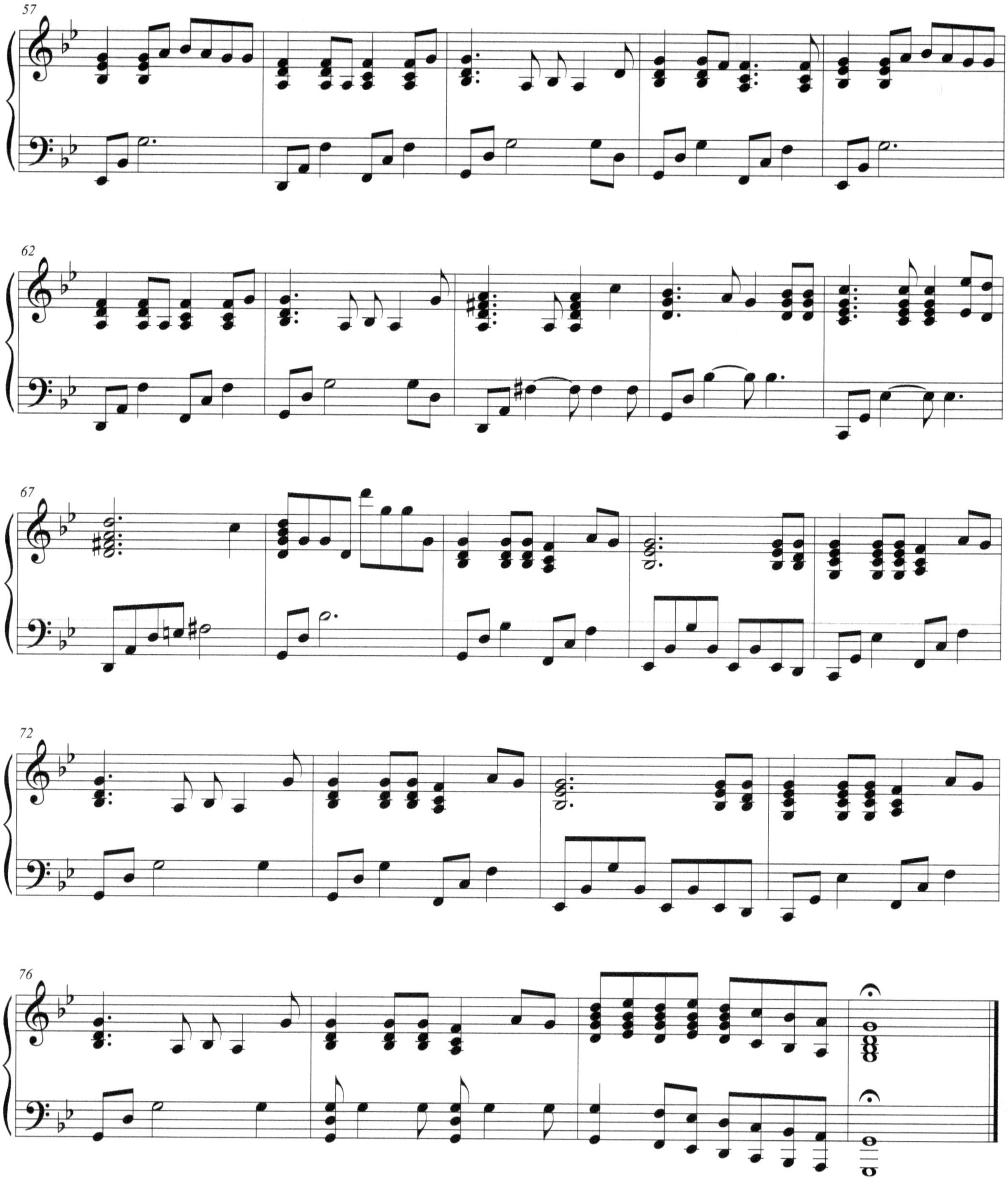
57
62
67
72
76

Clear My Mind

Eric Elder

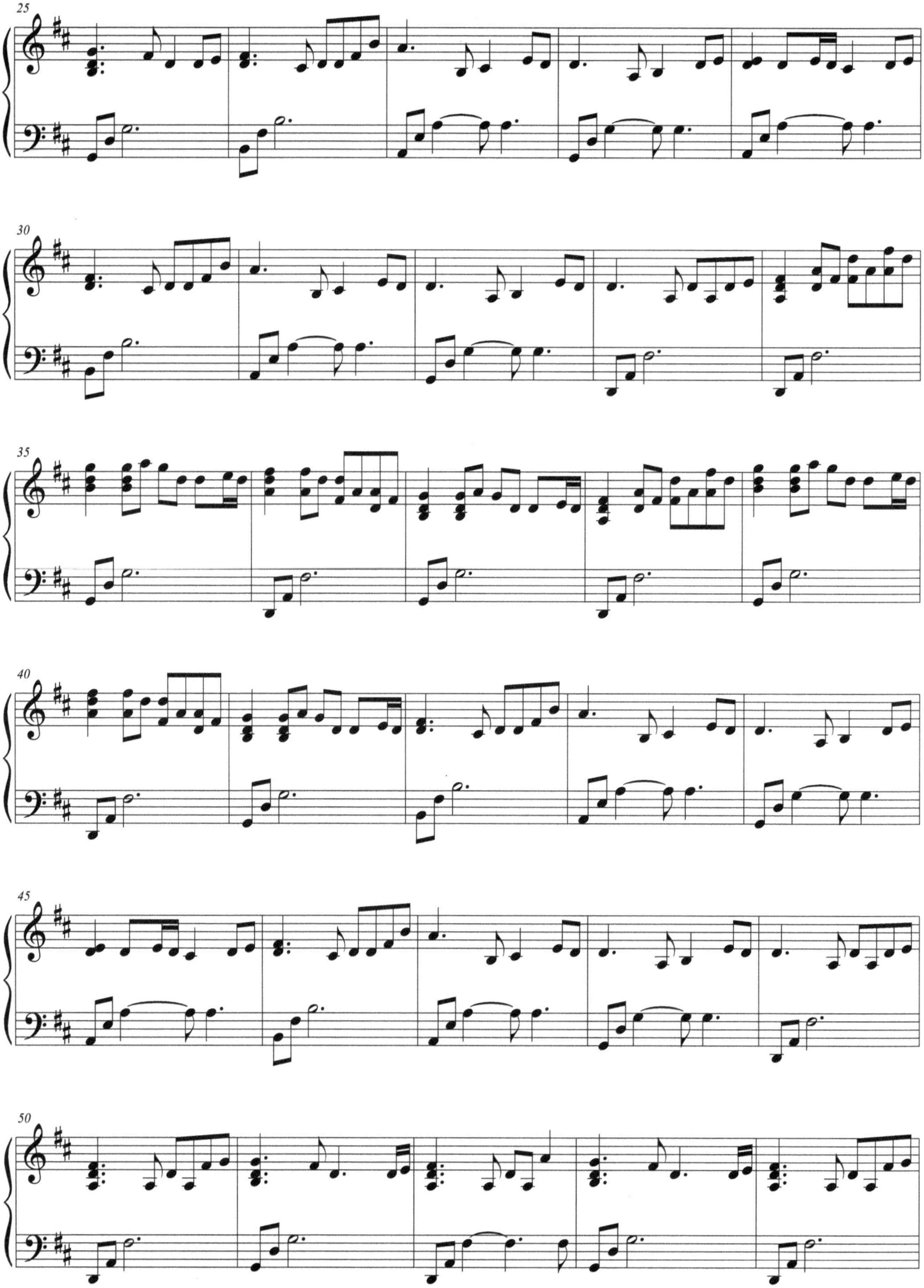
25
30
35
40
45
50

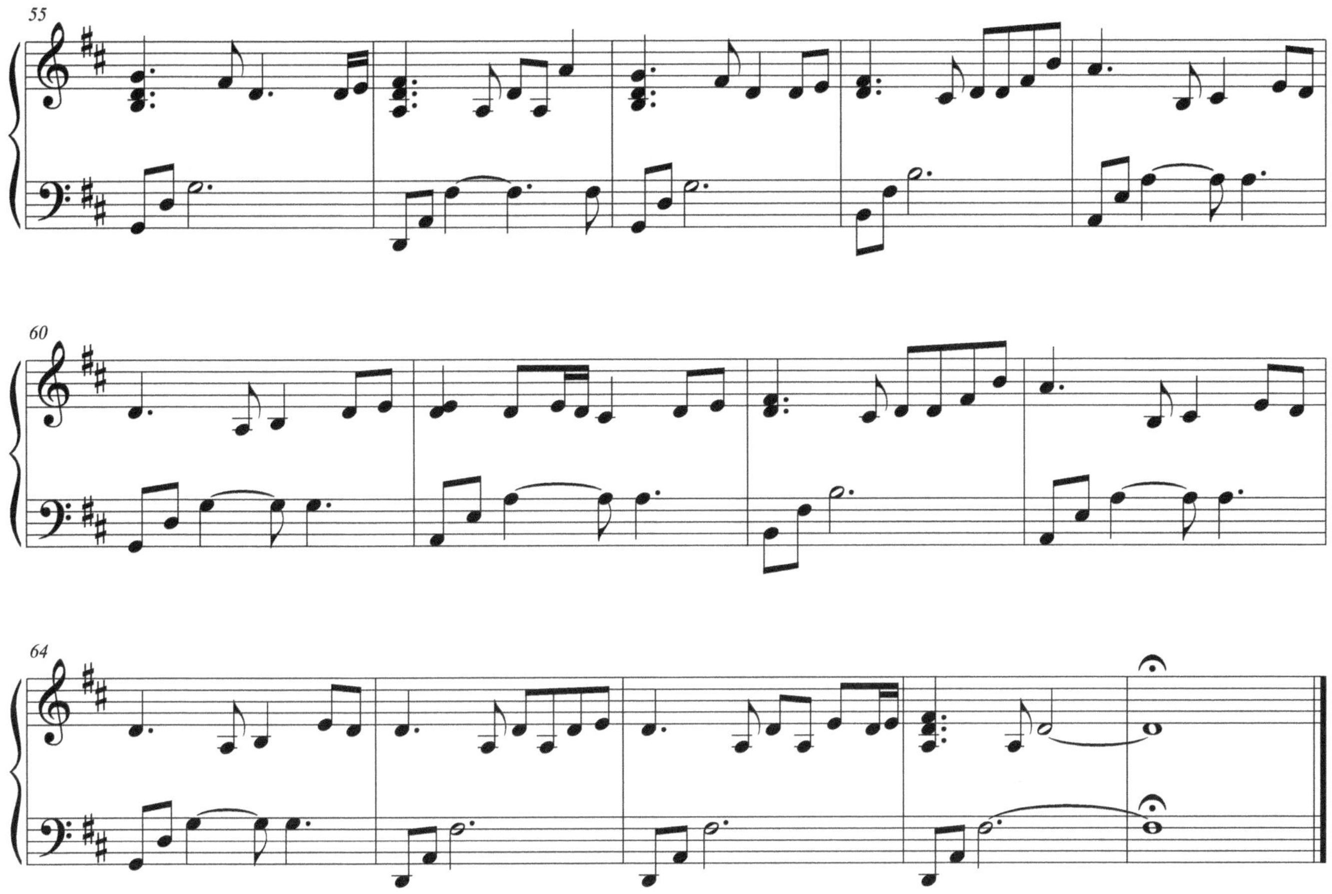
55
60
64

A Grand Man

Eric Elder

20

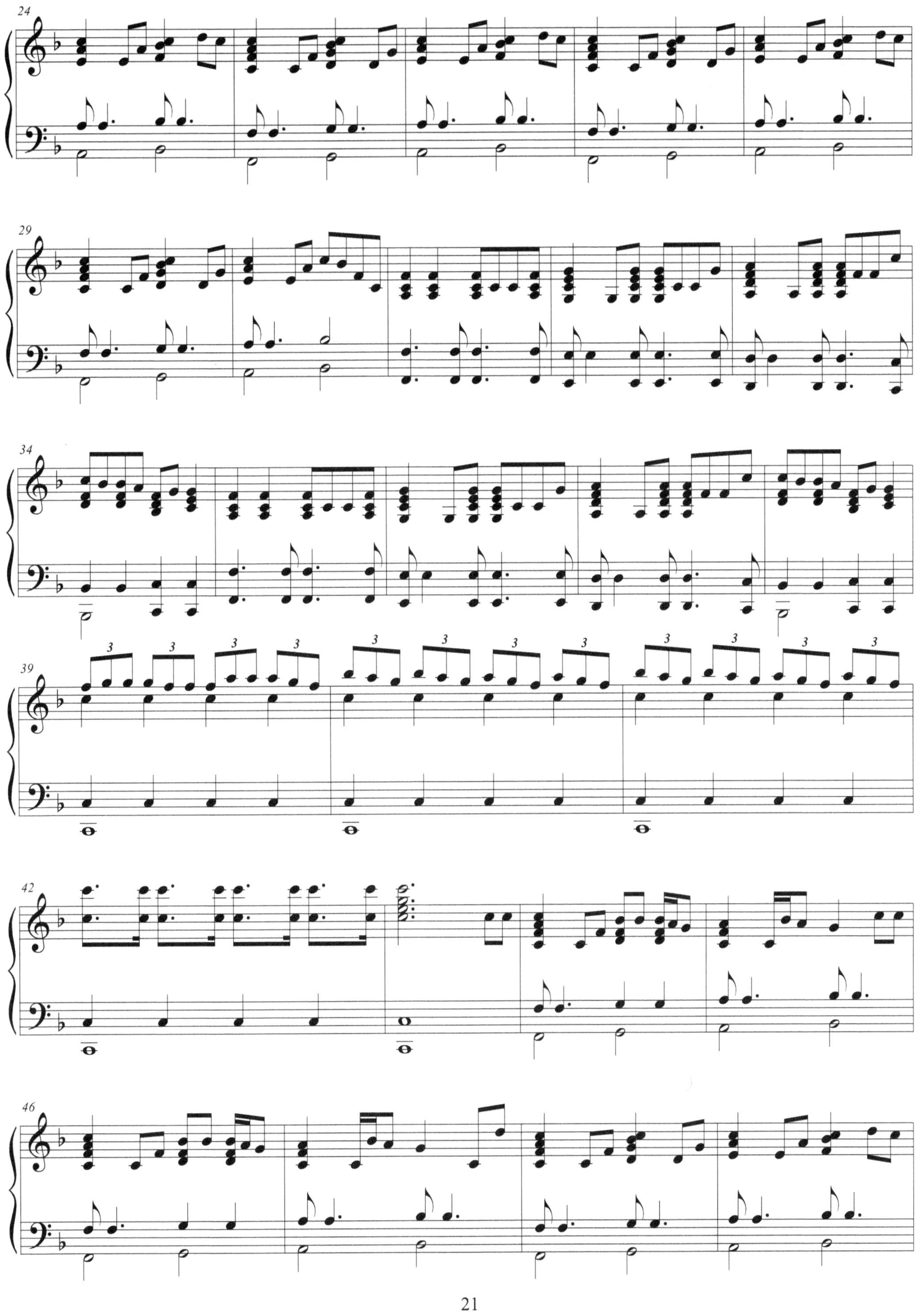
24
29
34
39
3
42
46

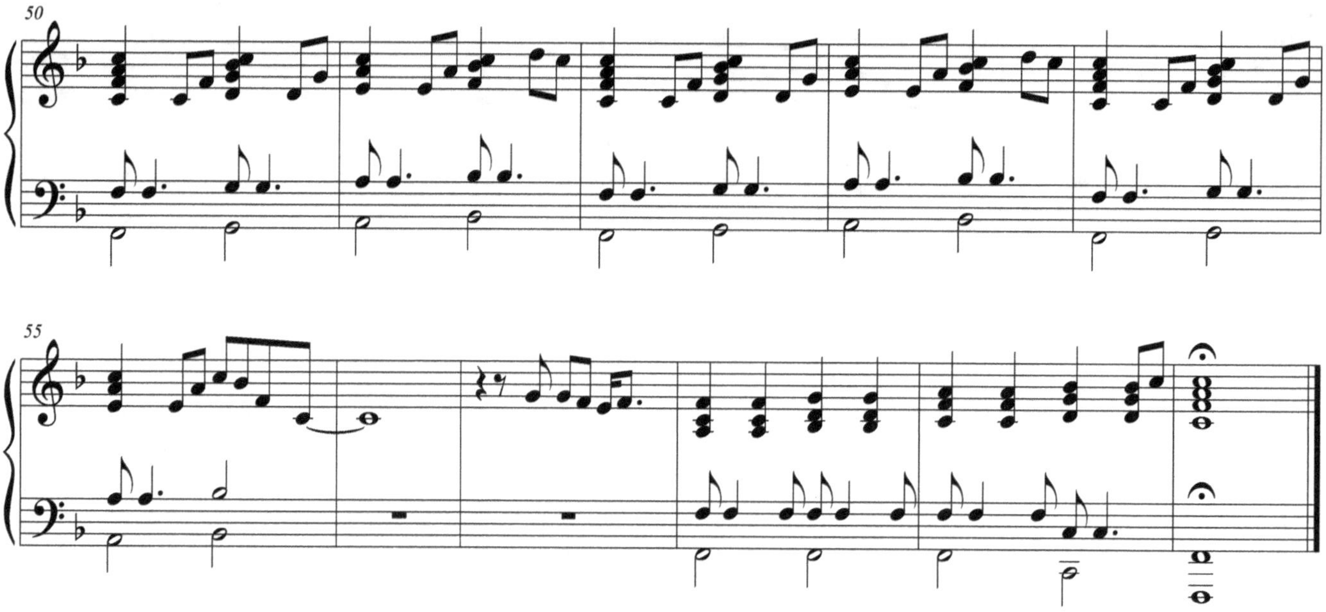
50
55

I Declare

Eric Elder

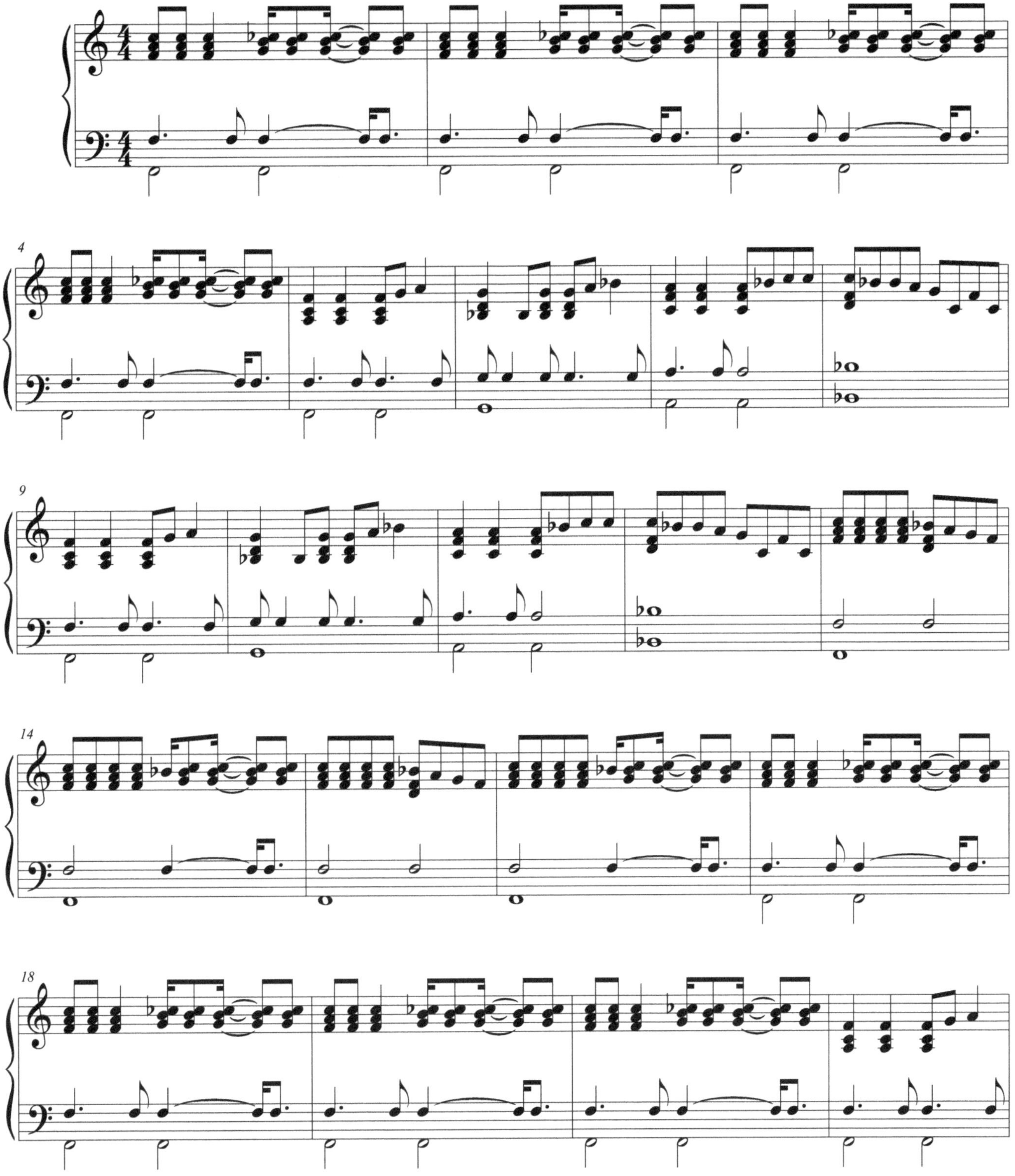

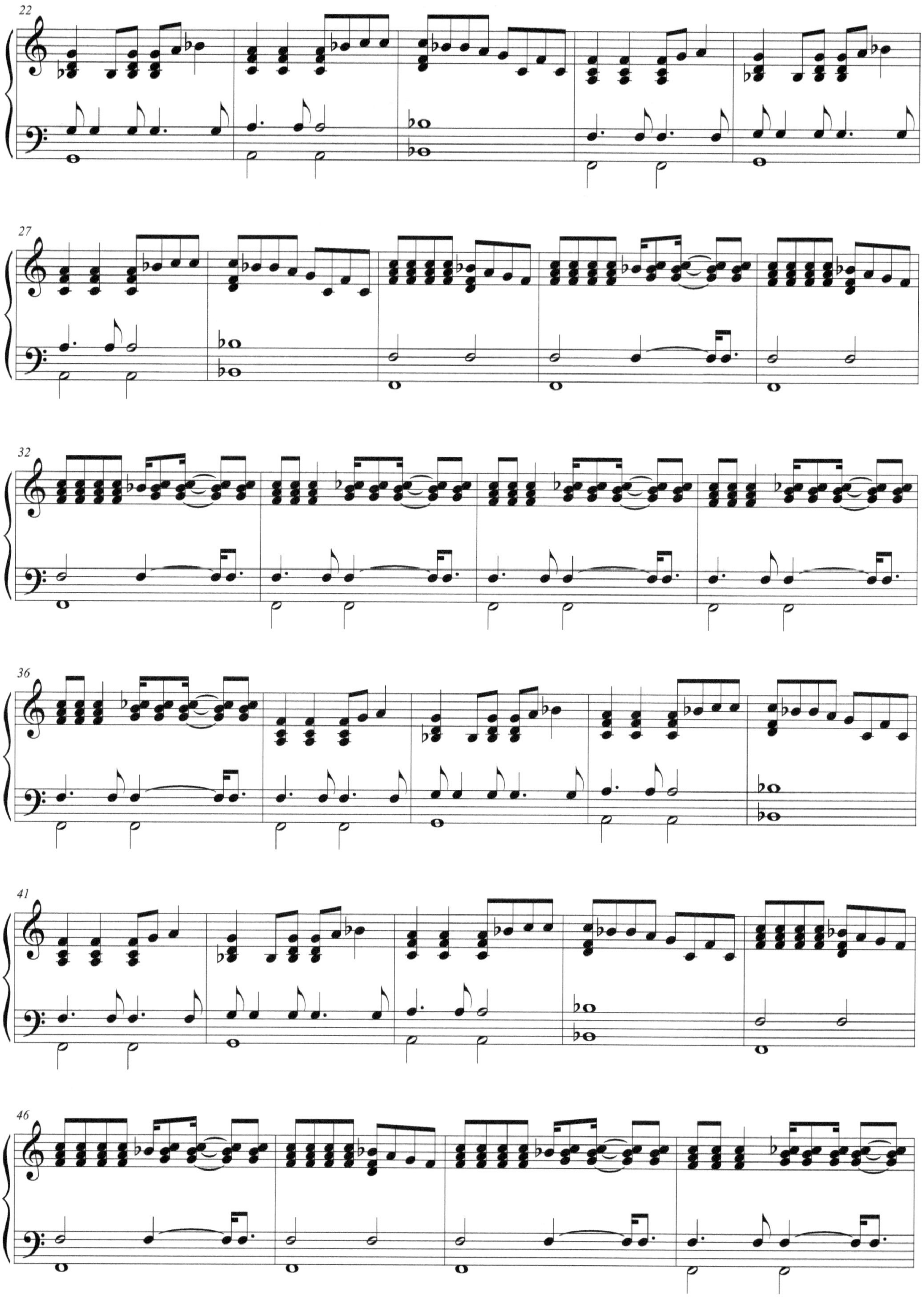
22
27
32
36
41
46

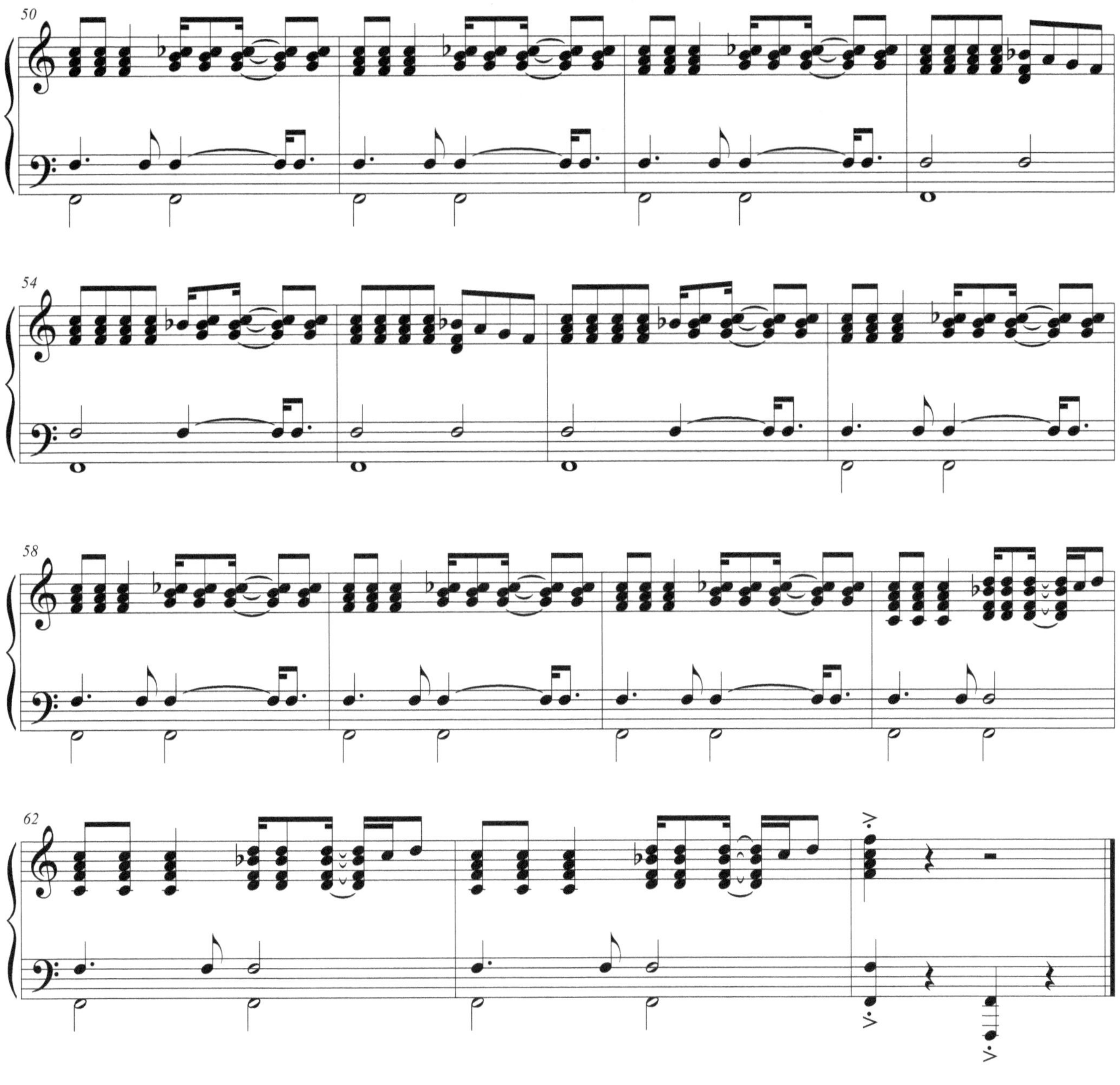
50
54
58
62

Trust Me

Eric Elder

26

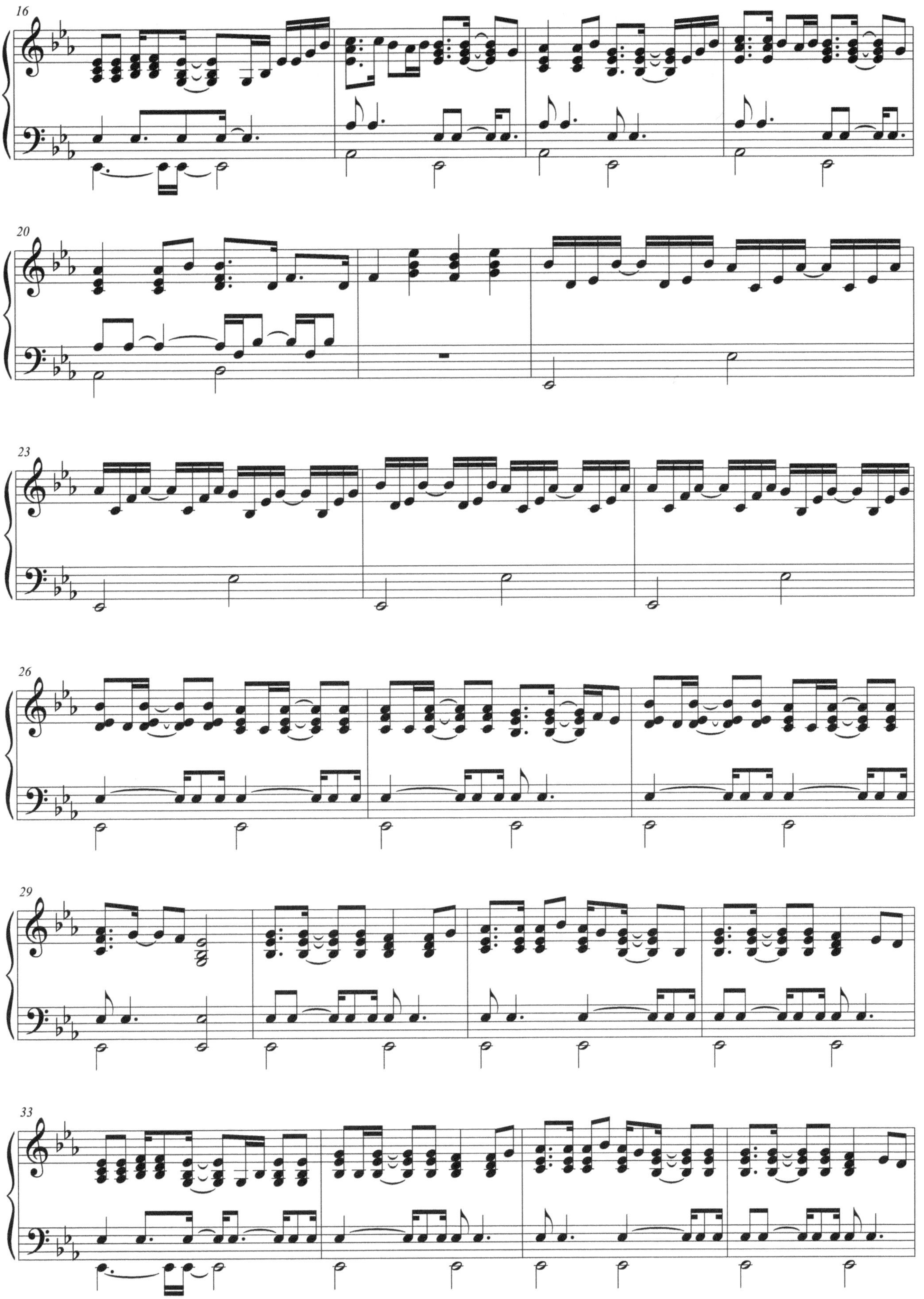
16
20
23
26
29
33

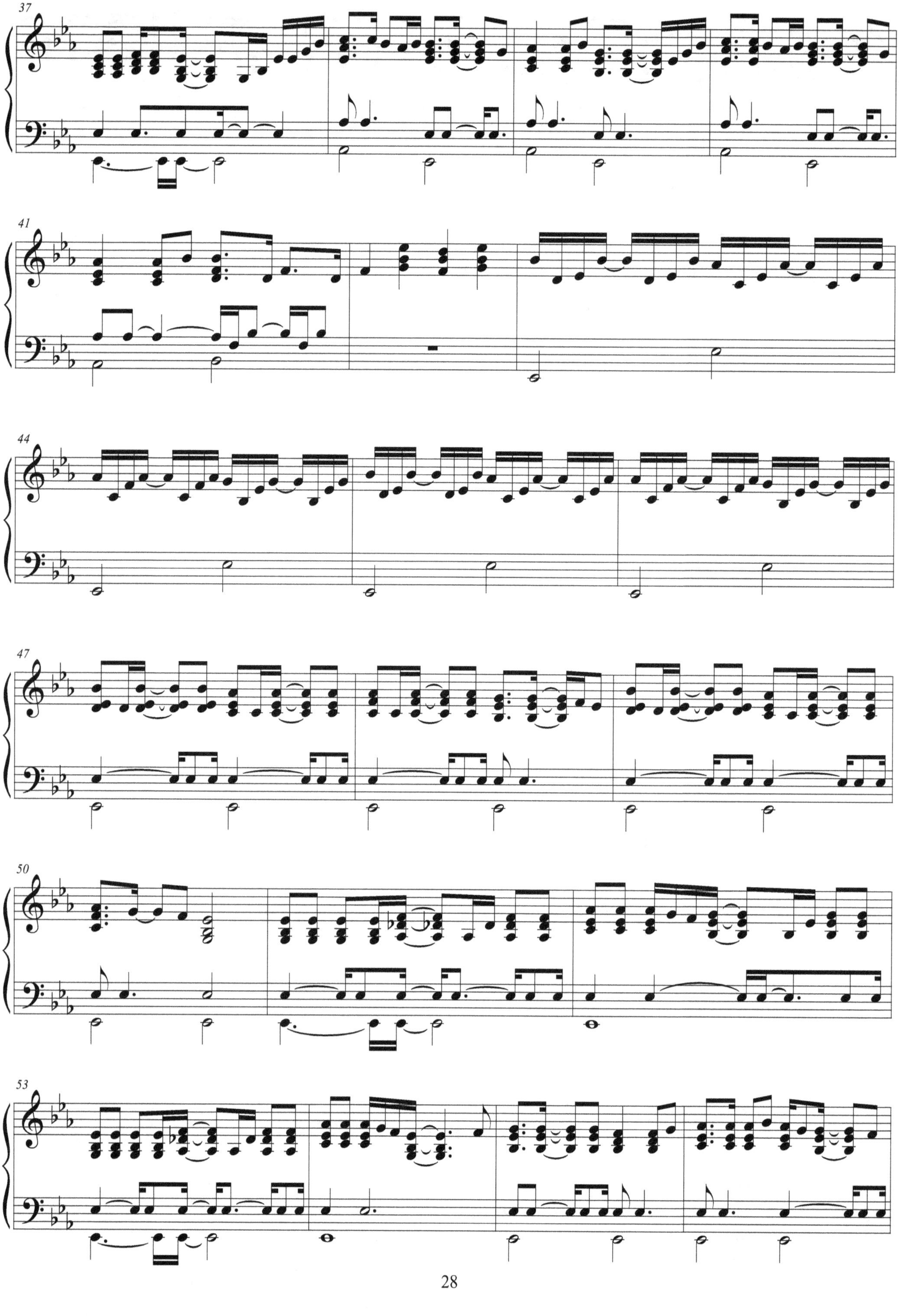
37
41
44
47
50
53

Trust Me

29

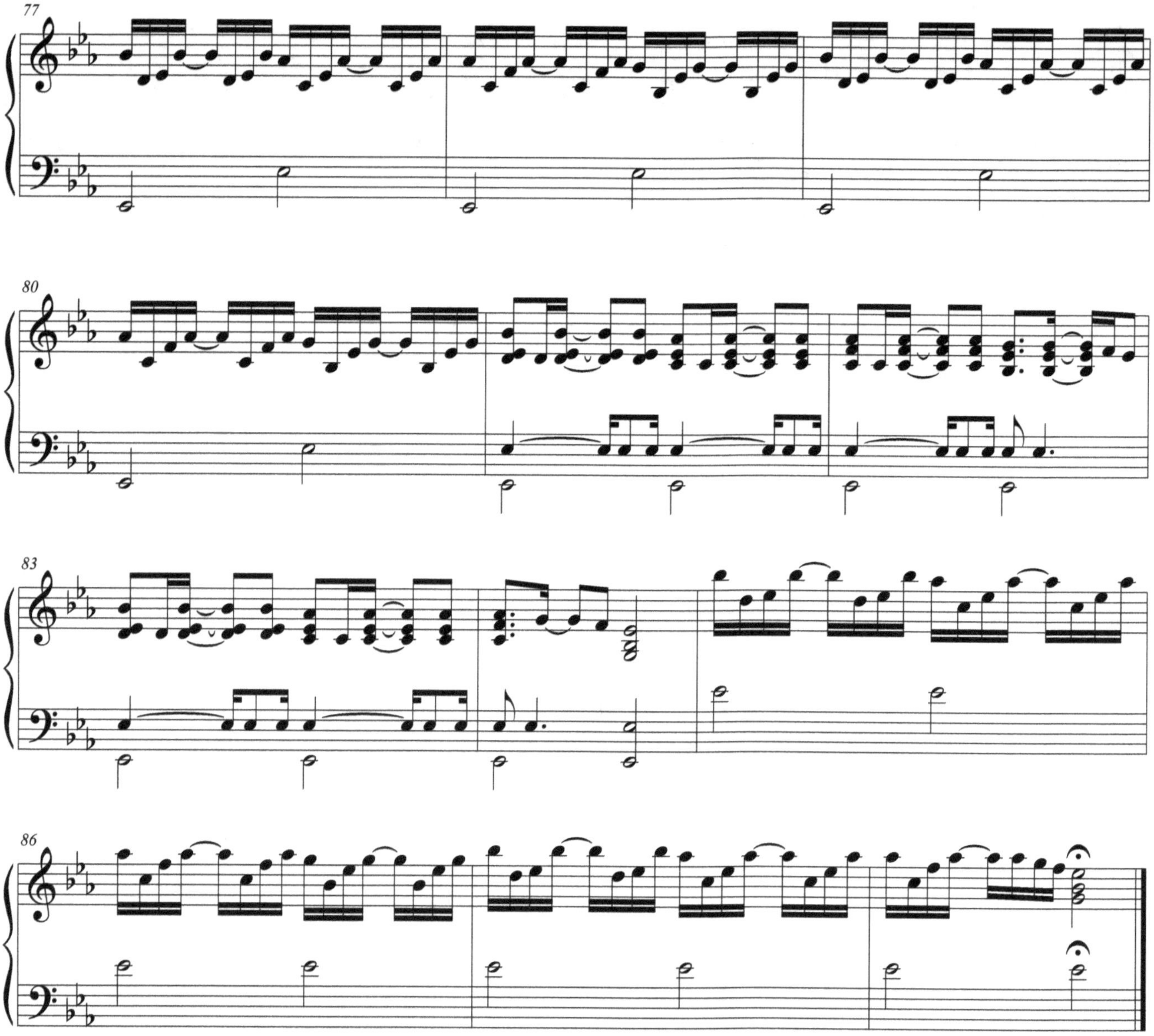
77
80
83
86

Lord, I Pray

Eric Elder

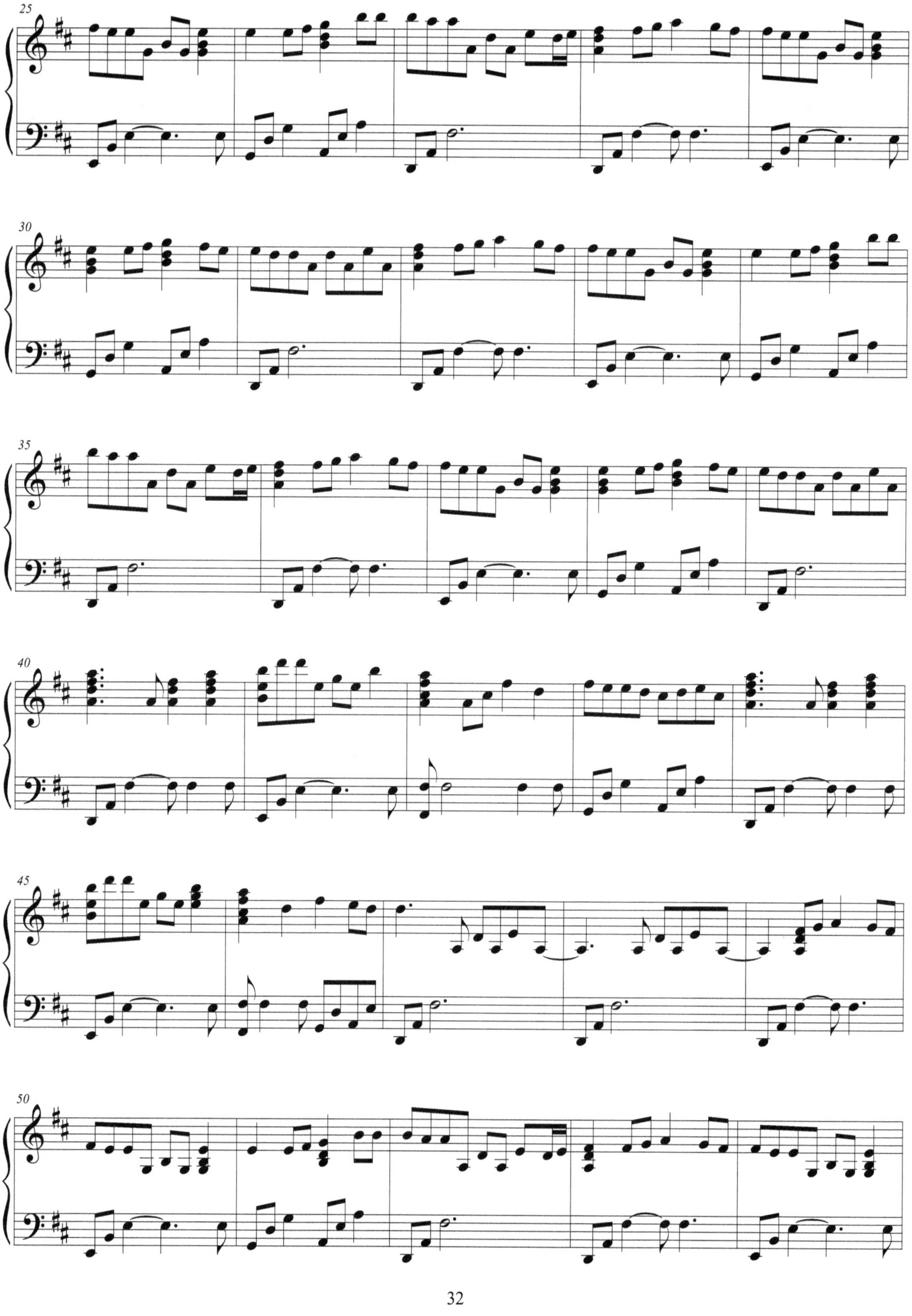
25
30
35
40
45
50

Lord, I Pray

My Lana

Eric Elder

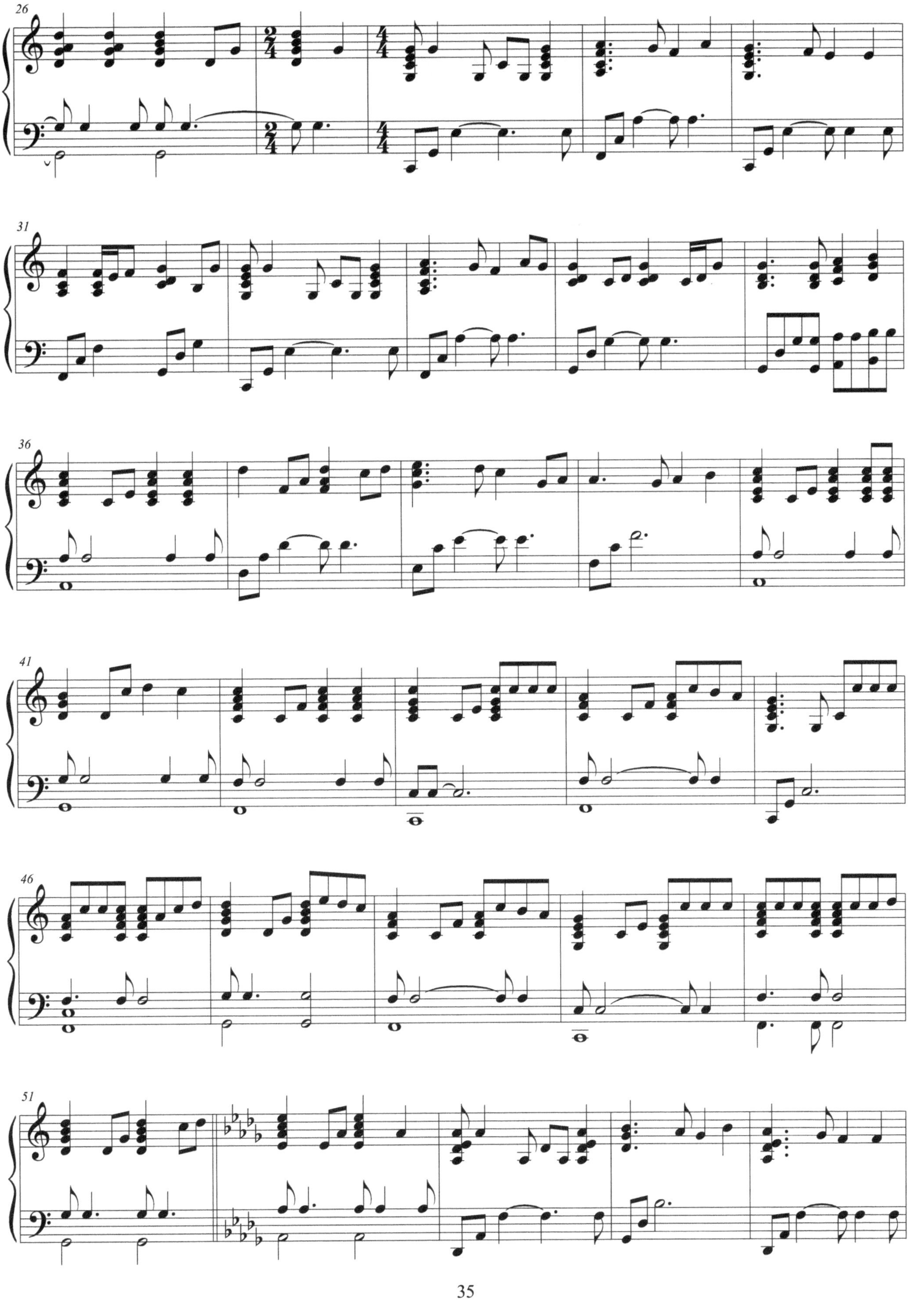
26
31
36
41
46
51

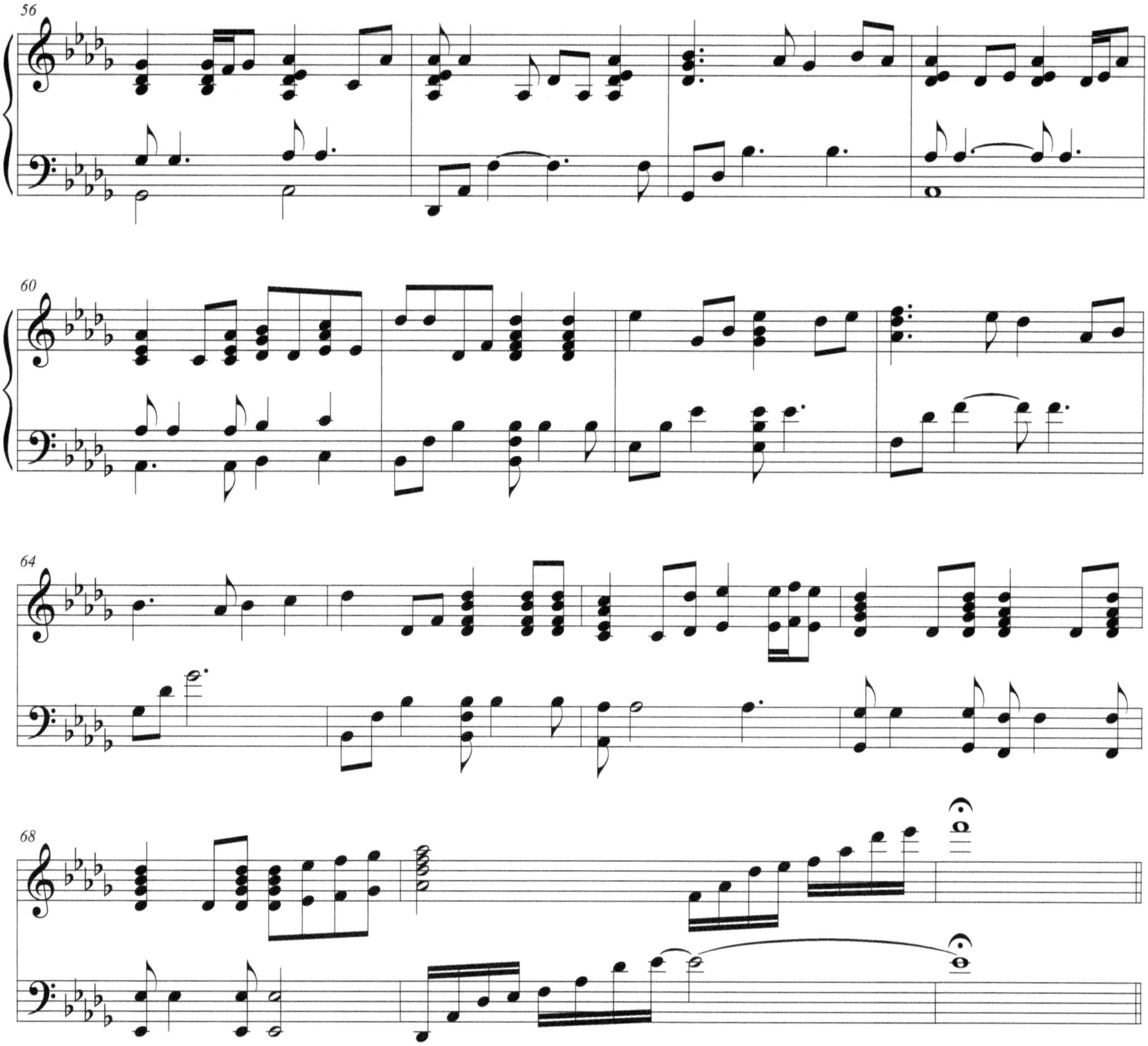
56
60
64
68

Blessed Are You

Eric Elder

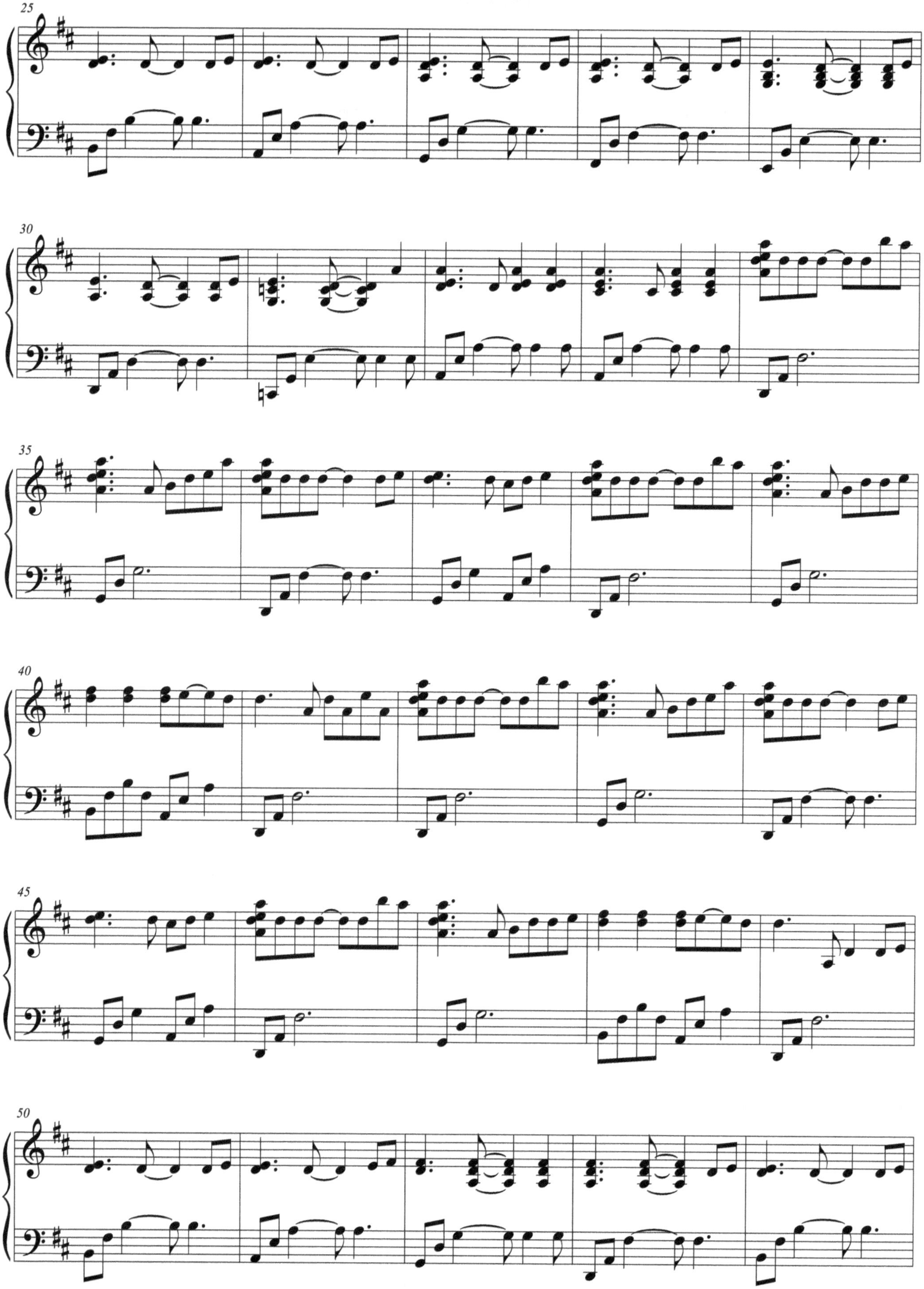
25
30
35
40
45
50

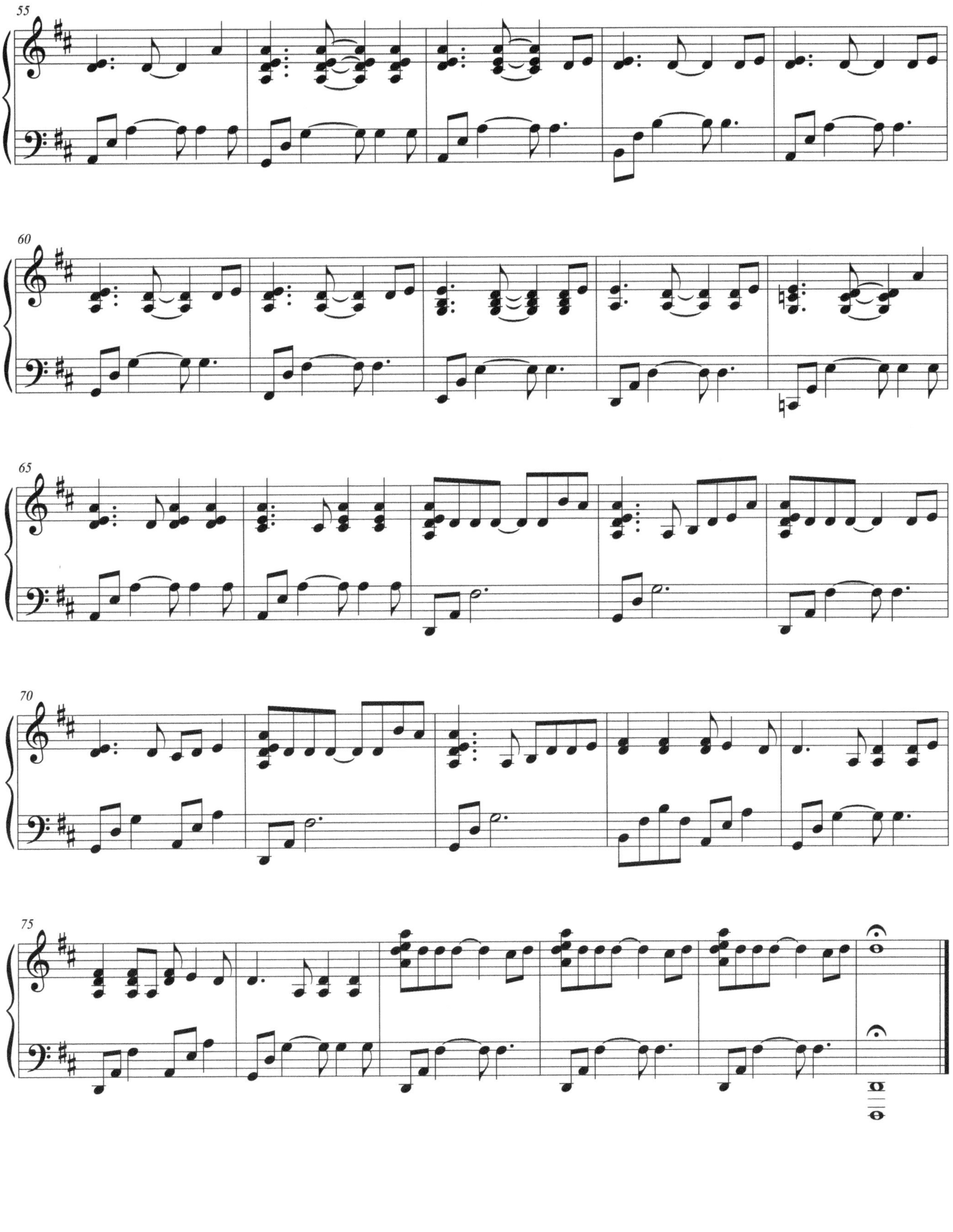
55
60
65
70
75

I've Seen The Sun

Eric Elder

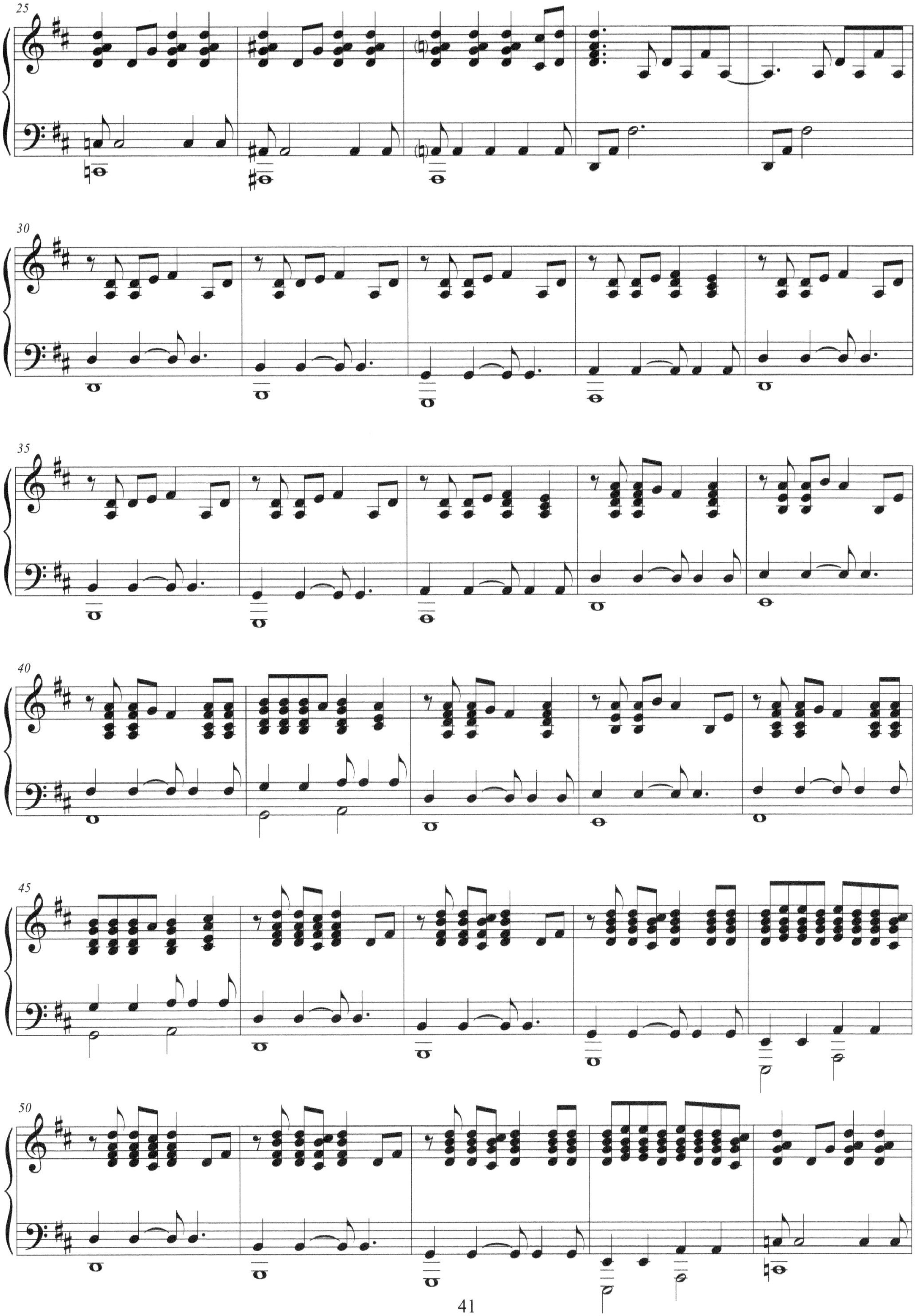
25
30
35
40
45
50

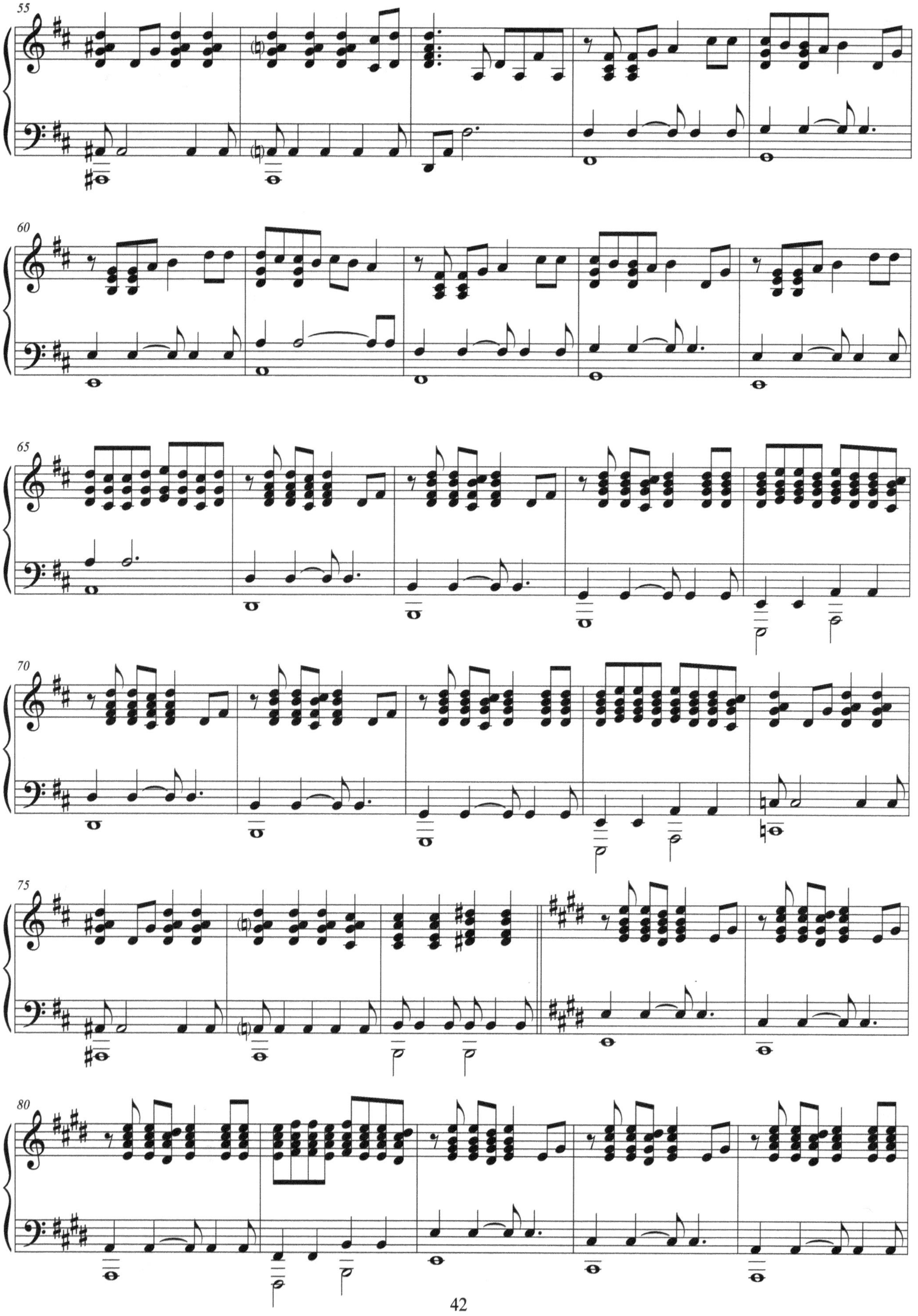
55
60
65
70
75
80

I've Seen The Sun

www.ingramcontent.com/pod-product-compliance
Lightning Source LLC
LaVergne TN
LVHW061249060426
835508LV00018B/1560